T0196887

GET A JOB IN TECHNOLOGY

Get a Job in Technology is your one-stop-shop to learning everything there is to know about working in tech… and the STEM subjects you need to get there!

From techno math to smartphone science, discover what computer engineers, video game designers and programmers need to know to do their jobs. Would you rather design a video game than build a cell phone? Explore your perfect career match, and dive into additional resources, classes and tips.

This book is a must-have for kids fascinated by awesome gadgets and the people who build them.

Matt Koceich is a public school teacher with the Mansfield Independent School District. He has a Master's degree in Education from the University of North Texas and has been teaching for twenty-five years. He and his family live in Texas.

GET A JOB IN TECHNOLOGY

A Kid's Guide to a Career in Cool Gadgets and Wacky Electrics

Matt Koceich

Routledge
Taylor & Francis Group

NEW YORK AND LONDON

Cover image: © Getty Images

First published 2023
by Routledge
605 Third Avenue, New York, NY 10158

and by Routledge
4 Park Square, Milton Park, Abingdon, Oxon, OX14 4RN

Routledge is an imprint of the Taylor & Francis Group, an informa business

Library of Congress Cataloging-in-Publication Data
A catalog record for this title has been requested

ISBN: 978-1-032-20305-8 (hbk)
ISBN: 978-1-032-20025-5 (pbk)
ISBN: 978-1-003-26314-2 (ebk)

DOI: 10.4324/9781003263142

Typeset in Palatino
by codeMantra

Contents

1

Help Wanted

By the time you reach your junior year of high school, you will have achieved so much. You will have passed so many tests and read so many books, and just thinking about all the homework you've done might make your brain hurt.

Be proud of all that you've done! But, there's still a big thing called college waiting for you and that's where your third year of high school comes in. That's the time when you should think about researching and visiting colleges to see which one you like the best. However, to do that, it will help if you have an idea of what kind of job you want when you graduate.

No pressure! Seriously.

Your school days are to learn about what you like and what your talents are. Out of the billions of people in the world, there is only one you. That makes you very special. Maybe you like to draw or read books. Perhaps science just excites you like nothing else. Or maybe you like to play video games and hang out with your friends. There could be a chance you love a lot of different things. Remember, you are unique and that's the awesome part.

That's where this book comes to the rescue. The goal of these pages is to not only give you helpful information about careers related to the tech industry, but to get you thinking about technology in a brand new way. Hopefully, by the time you finish exploring all the cool opportunities here, you will give serious consideration to landing a job in the technology field. Even if you get to the end and feel that technology is not what you're wired

DOI: 10.4324/9781003263142-1

for, there's plenty of websites and links to keep your engaged well beyond when you read the last page! So, if you're ready, let's go explore the cool world of technology!

GIVE ME A T!

When someone mentions the word *technology*, what is the first thing that comes to mind? An iPhone? TikTok? YouTube? Or maybe it's coding, circuits or computers. Whatever you think about technology, there's so much more! And when it comes to finding a career in the tech industry, the possibilities are truly endless.

You may not have given much thought to what you want to do when you're older. Or maybe you're rather certain what your future career will be. Whether you're sure of your career path or not, there's so much to learn about the tech world that you're in for a treat. You might discover a possible job that's just the right fit, or you might find a way to use your talents and future job desires in a company that has connections to technology.

In these pages, we'll explore a wide variety of careers that are connected to the tech world. A lot of them you've probably heard of before and some of them you might be reading about for the first time. To make the best use of your time, QR codes have been inserted throughout the book for you to scan and learn more about various aspects of technology. At the end, you'll find a section that lists colleges with degree plans that fit the tech job you're looking for.

It might be a good idea to go grab a pen or pencil and new notebook to keep track of your learning. You never know when you'll be reading something and have get a great idea! Taking notes or making doodles or drawings of your learning will help you connect more with the material. When there's a lot of information, it's easy to forget what you read, so jotting down your thoughts or pictures can help you remember what was important.

Ok. If you're ready, let's go!

Just to clarify, there are six types of technology: communication (television, Internet, cell phones), electrical (computers, AI, circuits, software), energy (solar panels, wind turbines, batteries), mechanical (manufacturing, heavy engineering), medical (diagnostics, pharmaceutical, surgical) and transportation (GPS, flight, vehicles). When it comes to thinking about careers, that's a lot of different areas to have a chance of landing one you really want.

To start, here's a list of the current top jobs in the technology field: data scientist, software developer, information security analyst, computer systems analyst, web developer, sales engineer, IT manager and computer research scientist (Williams, 2021). How many of them have you heard of before now? Let's take a brief look at a few of them and see if you find anything that resonates with your talents.

SOFTWARE DEVELOPER

Software developers invent all the cool applications we take for granted. For instance, that game you really love playing? A software developer helped design that. And when you get to school and turn on your computer and surf the web—software developers had a big part in that whole experience.

You might see your parents shopping online or making deposits into their bank account using their phone. Later, you might see your mom or dad checking the weather on their phone or even plugging in an address to get directions. As you think about your day, you can see that software developers are the brains behind the technologies we can't imagine living without.

The best software developers are creative and have the technical savvy to carry out innovative ideas. You might expect software developers to sit at their desks designing programs all day—and they do, but their job involves many more responsibilities. They could spend their days working on a client project and writing new code. But they could also be tasked with maintaining or improving the code for programs that are already up and running.

Software developers also check for bugs or glitches in software. And although the job does involve extreme concentration and chunks of uninterrupted time, software developers work with others a lot, including fellow developers, managers or clients. Developers have to be good problem solvers who possess strong analytical skills and the ability to think outside the box. Is this a job you might be interested in?

DATA SCIENTIST

Data scientists use technology to make insights from large amounts of data they collect. It's a field that includes statistics, quantitative reasoning and computer programming skills. On top of all that, you need to be good at talking to people so you can report your research findings and explain how they might solve bigger problems you're trying to solve.

While data science is still a new career field, employers are increasingly recognizing the value of professionals with this expertise. Today, you'll find data scientists working at a range of organizations, including tech startups, government agencies, large companies and research institutions.

Chris Holdgraf, Director of the nonprofit International Interactive Computing Collaboration, which helps researchers and educators run data science infrastructure in the cloud, started learning about data science as a graduate student at University of California, Berkeley. He taught himself coding, analytics and other skills that he thought would help him conduct neuroscience research.

While serving as a fellow at the university's Berkeley Institute for Data Science, Holdgraf collected data from electrodes placed directly onto the surface of patients' brains to learn more about how they hear. Feeding the data into computer programs he created, Holdgraf ran experiments, made observations and drew conclusions about the brain's response to different types of sounds. That's really cool. Like Mr. Holdgraf, you too could become a data scientist and come up with a really neat experiment of your own.

IT MANAGER

Computer and information systems managers, or information technology managers, are the people who help businesses stay on top of the most current technology. These important employees deliver short- and long-term visions for the company's technology needs.

IT managers have to get along with people. They are in constant contact with top executives, they have to plan upgrades of a company's existing software or hardware, and they have to negotiate with vendors for the service of current products or the purchase of new ones. IT managers are also responsible for installing and upgrading an organization's computer systems and protecting the office network from hackers and malware.

While the highest-profile jobs are in computer systems design, almost all companies need IT managers. Businesses like banks and insurance firms rely heavily on IT managers to get the job done as well as state and local governments. The health care industry is another area of jobs that needs good IT managers to make sure hospitals and doctors' offices are running smoothly.

INFORMATION SECURITY ANALYST

Information security analysts are like the security guards of information systems. Their job is to plan and execute security protocols that shield an organization's computer systems and networks from cyber attacks. They also work hard to prevent, monitor and respond to data breaches and cyber attacks, which are becoming more and more common in today's society.

COMPUTER SYSTEMS ANALYST

Computer systems analysts use their knowledge of information technology and business to design better computer systems for their clients. Their primary goal is to understand their client's business, whether it's an organization in Silicon Valley or a firm on Wall Street. They want to learn how the organization uses technology. Analysts will then research the best technologies to help the organization's overall computer system—the hardware, the software and the networks—run more efficiently and effectively.

These professionals also use their business skills to prepare a cost–benefit analysis for the upgrades. And if management approves the upgrades, computer systems analysts will oversee the installation of the new systems. They also test the systems and train their organization in them. Computer systems analysts are the men and women who troubleshoot problems when they arise. The good news is that the Bureau of Labor Statistics projects that an estimated 46,600 jobs should open up for people who want to get this kind of job.

COMPUTER NETWORK ARCHITECT

Computer network architects design, build and maintain a variety of data communication networks, from "cloud" infrastructures to smaller intranets. You probably know, but just in case you're not sure, the "cloud" is a series of servers and databases that are on the Internet and not your personal computer. Take a

Google doc, for example. Let's say you start typing your document at home. The document is saved to the "cloud" because you can go to school and open up the same document even though you're on a different computer! We have network architects to thank for this awesome invention.

Along with a host of technical skills, computer network architects also have a deep understanding of the company or organization's business plans and objectives. They also do everything from budgeting the network design and implementation to managing a staff.

As companies and firms expand their IT networks, they'll increasingly rely on these professionals to build new networks and upgrade existing ones. The popularity of cloud computing is also expected to drive the need for more computer network architects.

DATABASE ADMINISTRATOR

Database administrators are the people who set up databases according to a company's needs and make sure they operate efficiently. They will also fine-tune, upgrade and test modifications to the databases as needed.

With information so readily available in this era of apps, tablets and social media, data has become the new treasure organizations must protect and cherish. Database administrators are being tasked with implementing security measures to ensure sensitive data doesn't fall into the hands of people with bad intentions.

The job involves attention to detail and problem-solving. Communication skills are also important since database administrators often work as part of a team with computer programmers and managers.

WEB DEVELOPER

Web developers are the folks who create websites. Is that something you might be interested in? When these creative people do their jobs well, everything about a site seems to fit together perfectly, from the colors and graphics, to the images and special effects, to the ease of navigation.

Web developers work in Photoshop to create the overall design, while others will be in charge of writing the code in programming languages such as HTML and CSS. If this interests you, you will have to become knowledgeable of software programs, web applications and programming languages, as well as have a solid understanding of design principles. Work environments for web developers vary from large corporations or governments to small businesses. Sometime people do this job on the side to make extra money as part-time employment.

COMPUTER PROGRAMMER

Have you heard of C++ or Python? They're not grades and snakes, but computer languages that programmers use to get machines to do specific tasks.

Computer programmers write the code that allows software programs to run. So just like a boss tells an employee what to do, a programmer tells a computer what to do. Basically, they write directions in C++ and Python or another language, and the computer then follows the programmer's detailed instructions. In many cases, a programmer's work will start after a software developer or engineer passes off design specifications for a particular program. The programmer's job entails refining the ideas and solving the problems that arise while converting the program into code.

Programmers can also rewrite, debug, maintain and test (and retest and retest) software and programs that instruct the computer to store or retrieve data, so the computer can perform better and more efficiently.

Computer programming is an exciting industry that will always be available to you as a good job opportunity after college.

The people who created Google are billionaires because they made it easy to search the Internet for just about any topic we can imagine. Today, our personal devices have more computing power than was available to launch all of the Apollo missions that landed men on the moon! Scan the QR code to check out a cool video that explains how a Google search works. It truly is an amazing process!

 This chapter has covered a lot of cool jobs that have something to do with technology. Was there one in particular that resonated with you? Remember, it's okay if you're not sure. Think about how to connect your talents with different aspects of careers and before you know it you'll be on your way to finding the job you were born to do!

Did you jot anything down in your notebook? Why don't you take a second and draw a picture of something in this chapter that really caught your attention? It would be fun to make notes in the margins of your picture about how you could use your talents to upgrade what's already being done.

One quick note before we move on. By now, you've probably heard of STEM (science, technology, engineering and math). Schools make sure to focus on these subjects because they know how important they are to students. For example, if you're thinking about becoming a software developer, you have to earn a Computer Science degree or something similar in a STEM discipline. In the next chapter, we're going to start with *science* and zero in on how specifically it is used in the tech industry.

2

Systems Science

When you think of science class, what comes to mind? Water cycle? Plant cells? Planets? Beakers and bar graphs? There's physical science, life science, Earth and space science, investigations and tons of question asking.

When it comes to technology, the smartphone seems to be the one thing that everyone can agree on as the tool that makes life so much easier. Let's take a look at the science behind that marvelous piece of technology.

HISTORY OF THE SMARTPHONE

Where did it all begin? In 1947, the seed that would eventually grow into smartphones first took root. It didn't look impressive, at least not next to the flashier rockets for outer space that other scientists and engineers were building at the same time, but it was important nonetheless (Uswitch, 2021).

Three scientists at AT&T's Bell Laboratories in New Jersey were tinkering with a device that would turn an electrical signal on and off. The dime-sized contraption, pieced together out of germanium and gold, turned out to be the reason why you can get texts from a friend halfway around the world, look up videos on YouTube on your phone and take advantage of your favorite social media sites (Bellis, 2019).

DOI: 10.4324/9781003263142-2

Today, we know this device as the transistor. Transistors form the basis of modern electronics; we stamp out millions at a time, and they could all fit on the end of a pin. The transistor literally changed the world.

Before the transistor, TVs and radios ran on vacuum tubes. These were hard to manufacture and hard to miniaturize because they depend on maintaining a perfect vacuum, but then 1947 came around and with it the transistor.

Once transistors took off, electronics never looked back. Scientists quickly figured out that silicon was the perfect material for transistors—it made cheap, precise and miniature devices. In the latter half of the twentieth century, the potential for better electronics seemed virtually limitless.

In 1965 a scientist named Gordon Moore predicted that the number of transistors on a computer chip would double every two years, and Moore's Law has been remarkably accurate through to the present day (Gianfagna, 2021).

As transistors got smaller and smaller, computers performed more and more calculations per second. This let engineers pack unbelievable computing power into smaller platforms. Silicon transistors are why computers could go from the monsters that occupied entire rooms in the 1940s into the small devices we enjoy today. The tiniest transistors are now less than thirty nanometers long which means you could fit 16,000 of them, side-by-side, in the period at the end of this sentence (Riordan, 2020).

Think of a transistor as an on/off switch. When it's "on," it allows current to flow through. When it's "off," the current stops. This is the language of computers: 1 (on) and 0 (off). As they get smaller, silicon transistors get less efficient. The barriers separating "on" from "off" are so thin that the transistor never quite turns completely off, and it starts to leak power. It's like trying to dam a stream of water with your hand; most of the water stops, but a little still trickles through. Scan the QR code to check out a cool video that explains just how awesome this tech invention is!

In electronics, power is lost as heat; leaky transistors are one reason why laptops run so hot. Much of the engineering in computers, from your phone to the largest supercomputers, revolves around cooling the chips. In fact, in terms of watts emitted per square inch, a transistor is comparable to a nuclear reactor. "At some point, we'll hit the limit, and we won't be able to cool the transistors fast enough," said Anand Bhattacharya, a physicist at Argonne. "The answer almost certainly lies in a new class of materials to replace transistors." Transistors, and everything else in your smartphone, are the domain of a field called "materials science" (Argonne National Laboratory, 2013).

SAY WHAT?

Materials science is the field that takes discoveries in physics and chemistry and uses them to arrange atoms to do what we want them to do. Blacksmiths, among the earliest materials scientists, melted iron and charcoal together to make steel. Egyptian materials scientists found that melting sand and alkaline made glass (Kukich et al., 2018).

New materials transform the world. We categorize our past according to what materials we could make: the Stone Age, the Bronze Age, the Atomic Age. The hunt for the next round of miracle materials will give us faster, cheaper and smarter electronics, as well as everything from affordable solar panels to batteries that power cars for 300 miles.

Inventing a material today is a bit more complex than it used to be. Our electronics have gotten so sophisticated that in order to create a new material, we have to know what it looks like in incredibly fine detail—at the level of molecules and atoms. To do so, scientists have several ways of getting pictures of what's happening down there, even though it's far too small for human eyes to see.

One way is to shoot incredibly powerful X-rays at a sample. When the beams hit and scatter in all directions, scientists piece together the information to recreate a "picture" of the material at nearly atomic detail.

Sophisticated computer models can predict behaviors of unknown materials; running them on a supercomputer, like the IBM Blue Gene/Q Mira, lets scientists combine millions of data points for the most accurate models. They run thousands of simulations of different ways to combine chemicals. Once the computer spits out a few interesting answers, they can take those to the lab to confirm the results.

Oxides

Scientists are also looking at interesting materials called Mott insulators, which could eventually replace silicon. Mott insulators are a curious class of materials. Conventional theory predicts that they should conduct electricity, but when scientists tested them, they found the materials were actually insulators. Many in the field believe that if we could find the right recipe, we could build Mott insulators that flip back and forth between conducting and insulating when a voltage is applied.

The problem is that people don't understand the basic physics behind Mott insulators nearly as well as they do silicon; scientists don't yet know enough about them to harness their power.

Until last year, no one had built a working Mott-based transistor. A team of Japanese scientists managed to build a prototype in 2012, which set the materials world buzzing, but it only worked partially, and the conditions they used aren't really practical for a working smartphone or computer (Argonne National Laboratory, 2013). This could be one area that you could research as you get older and see if you have any cool breakthroughs. You never know!

Mott insulators are made out of transition metal oxides: metals from a particular section of the periodic table (like copper, manganese or iron) with oxygen added.

Oxides can do things that silicon can't, like change to be magnetic or not magnetic, which could represent "on" and "off" and eventually replace the transistor.

Magnets

Magnets are already the magic behind loudspeakers, from the tiny ones inside earbuds to the big ones in amps at concerts. But if experiments pan out, they might become the backbone of electronic computing as well.

Magnets have all sorts of interesting properties for electronics because they are nonvolatile which means they don't use power to maintain stored information.

Teeny Machines

When you tilt your phone sideways, the picture re-orients itself along with you. How does your phone know to do that? There are these microscopic machines that sense the change in speed as you tilt the phone and relay the message to the phone's brain. The phone's compass, microphone and clock all use these tiny machines called microelectromechanical systems, or MEMS. Some are even small enough to be called *nano* electromechanical systems (NEMS).

MEMS are tiny mechanical machines, usually made out of silicon, that run in the neighborhood of ten microns long—the diameter of a single red blood cell. NEMS are even smaller. MEMS are interesting because they let electronics do all sorts of interesting things that transistors alone can't do. For example, the device that tells the phone it's being tilted is called an accelerometer.

MEMS are all over, like in your car's airbags to sense crashes the instant they happen. They also pick up data to activate anti-lock brakes. Many laptops have MEMS accelerometers that detect a sudden change in altitude (i.e., when the laptop is dropped) and adjust the hard drive in midair to prevent damage.

Our phones may be smarter today than fifty years ago, but like the three scientists at Bell Laboratories in 1947, we still look to the future and wonder what they'll be able to do after another fifty years of research. That's where you come in. As you learn more, you might discover the next big thing when it comes to electronics. Don't stop reading and learning!

Δ

There are so many options to choose from when considering a career in technology. It might be helpful to mark your place here, and grab your notebook and journal your thoughts and ideas about how science and technology go together.

Draw pictures. Jot down ideas. Concepts. Make it your own.

Remember whether you love science, or maybe up to now it wasn't on your list of favorite school subjects, that your future might involve a career in the tech field. Either way, all the opportunities to get involved with science in smartphones really make it a subject to pay attention to.

Don't forget, you are special and unique, so whatever you put your mind to, you will be able to add new things and ideas! Spend time thinking about what you would like to research about the science behind smartphones. You never know. One day you might have the chance to make your ideas come true and invent the next generation of devices.

In the next chapter, we're going to investigate ways that technology is used for tech-related jobs. Ready? Let's go!

3

Techy Technology

When it comes to technology, the possibilities are endless. Sometimes people think of technology as the bits and pieces that go into a smartphone to make it "smart." If you're keeping a journal to record your thoughts about possible careers in technology you might like to pursue when you're older, start a new section for the way your talents or ideas might line up with the information provided here in Chapter 3.

Let's explore some awesome things that make our everyday lives easier to see how technology is used to get things done. You've no doubt heard of all of them, but as you go through the list, think of ways you could improve on the existing technologies to make them even more useful!

WEBSITES

The Internet is itself the function of multiple pieces of digital technology, and websites are one of the most common ways that people access it. As you know, websites give people all sorts of information and are interactive—for example, not only can you see what movies are playing at your theater, but you can buy your tickets online, too.

DOI: 10.4324/9781003263142-3

BUYING AND SELLING ONLINE

Online shopping (can you say Amazon?) continues to skyrocket and gives people thousands of choices. You can buy from a large retailer at the other end of the country, or from an individual in your home town. Likewise, selling online is easy too. Do you have any ideas of how to create even more opportunities for people in this area?

SMARTPHONES

Mobile phones revolutionized communication, especially through the creation of texting. Now we have smartphones, which incorporate many other types of digital technology such as cameras, calculators and mapping. Let's take a look at how one phone in particular changed our lives forever.

APPLE IPHONE

Though it wasn't the first smartphone, Apple really made a statement when it introduced the iPhone in 2007. Social media, messaging and the mobile Internet wouldn't be nearly as powerful or universal if they hadn't been optimized for the iPhone and its competitors.

Armed with powerful features and able to run thousands of apps, they squeezed more functionality into one device than ever before. The mobile phone revolution brought the death of technology such as point-and-shoot cameras, dashboard GPS units, camcorders, PDAs and MP3 players.

Now, fifteen years after the iPhone's introduction, more than 3.5 billion people around the world use a smartphone, nearly half

 the Earth's population! One of the coolest parts of the smartphone is the touchscreen (Hanson, 2021). All of that power at the touch of a finger. Scan the QR code to learn just how amazing the technology is behind this invention!

DIGITAL TELEVISION

Digital technology has transformed televisions in numerous ways. Both picture and audio quality have undergone dramatic improvements. Modern TVs can also stream movies and shows, rather than just receive programs via an antenna or cable connection.

VIDEO STREAMING

Video streaming can be used for numerous purposes. You can watch movies or shows online. You can chat with people online and see them live using applications such as Skype, Zoom and Teams. You can watch or stream live events using live streaming. Sites like YouTube provide numerous other viewing options for information or entertainment. Streaming technology can increasingly be accessed through a variety of devices, including computers, televisions and smartphones.

EBOOKS

Digital alternatives to traditional print books are now all over. This enables users to access a multitude of reading materials from a single, portable device, so there's no longer the same need to carry around a lot of bulky, heavy books. It's easy to alter the font size and style to suit reader preferences. Many people like this option because, unlike with print books, there are no trees cut down to make digital books.

DIGITAL MUSIC

Digital audio arrived for consumers in the shape of compact disks, providing much greater sound quality than traditional analog. Today, most music listeners stream their audio from sites like Spotify which is a digital music, podcast and video service that gives its users access to millions of songs and other content from creators all over the world!

GEOLOCATION

The combination of satellite and digital technology means that the location of a device, such as a mobile phone, GPS device, or Internet-connected computer, can be calculated very accurately. This information can then be used with other digital applications, such as mapping technology, to provide users with relevant information related to their location.

Apps like Waze and Google Maps help drivers know where to go and the fastest routes to get there through the use of geolocation technology.

VLOGS

Digital technology had enabled the creation of blogs, which sprouted up all across the web for years. With the increase of smartphone technology, these were joined by video blogs (vlogs), which often contain personal reflections, advice and random thoughts. They are also increasingly interactive, containing links to videos and other media, and are often accompanied by readers' / viewers' comments.

SOCIAL MEDIA

Social media platforms, such as Facebook, TikTok and Instagram, have seen an explosion in popularity in recent years. They bring together multiple pieces of digital technology to enable users to interact via text, photos, video, as well as form social groups. Social media applications rely almost entirely on user-generated content.

COMPUTERS

Laptops, tablets, desktops and other forms of computers depend upon digital technology to function. Originally computers were huge and used mainly by large companies and scientific projects for performing complex calculations and storing large amounts of information. Nowadays, they are much more compact, as well as powerful, and can perform a multitude of tasks.

PRINTERS

Printers are another digital device that are so commonplace nowadays that we pretty much take them for granted. Although information increasingly tends to be stored rather than printed, life without these output devices would still be difficult to imagine. We also shouldn't forget 3D printers, which are increasingly presenting both new opportunities and challenges.

3D PRINTING

3D printing is the process of synthesizing a three-dimensional object. We've seen the concept play out on TV and in movies for years, and now with home 3D printers it's finally growing beyond a wildly exotic hobby for a small enthusiast audience.

3D printing got an early foothold as a way to design prototypes of just about anything. The technology allows manufacturers to build plastic components that are lighter than metal alternatives and with unusual shapes that can't be made by conventional injection molding methods.

The devices are used to create materials inside football helmets and Adidas running shoes, and Porsche plans to roll out a new 3D printing program that will allow customers to have their cars' seats partially 3D-printed!

SELF-SCAN MACHINES

These machines have become increasingly common as they become more sophisticated and scanning technology such as RFID gradually replaces barcodes. Common examples include self-scanning of shopping products when buying at a store, and going through passport control in certain international airports.

ATMS

ATMs were invented in London in 1967 and since then have given people a quick and easy way to access their bank accounts. Modern ATMs can be used for such things as cash withdrawals, checking bank balances and depositing money without having to wait until the bank opens.

DIGITAL CAMERAS

These devices have much greater versatility than traditional cameras, especially when used in conjunction with other digital technology. Digital images are easier to store, organize, edit, email and print. Most digital cameras can capture video too.

CARS AND OTHER VEHICLES

Modern cars have computers at their core to monitor and adjust the engine and control safety systems, as well as operate comfort, convenience and security systems. Other vehicles such as boats and aircraft rely even more heavily on computers for their functionality. As technology continues to develop, it is only a matter of time before self-driving vehicles become the norm.

ALARM CLOCKS

Digital clocks have a number of advantages over traditional analog clocks: they don't make a ticking sound; they are easy to read, even in the dark; and the alarms go off at the precise time that you set them. They can also be combined with music, so that you wake up to your favorite playlist.

ROBOTICS

As digital robotic technology becomes more sophisticated, it becomes more widely used. Robotic machines can already be commonly found in the manufacturing industry. They are also used for tasks that are dangerous to humans, such as detecting and defusing bombs. Scientists are also working on nanorobots, tiny robots that could for example be injected into the human body to carry out medical investigations and procedures.

DRONES AND GUIDED MISSILES

There are many military uses for digital technology. Drones (unmanned combat aerial vehicles) and guided missiles incorporate digital technology in order to operate effectively. Drones are typically directed in real time by a remote human controller. Missiles use digital technology for their guidance, targeting and flight systems.

BANKING AND FINANCES

Many people now do most of their banking either on their computer or their phone. There are apps your parents have access to for a range of other things too, such as checking credit scores, or paying credit card bills. Apps such as PayPal and Venmo allow people to transfer money, take payments and pay bills. This saves your parents a ton of gas money because they don't have to drive across town to deposit checks anymore.

WI-FI

The smartphone and the Internet we use today wouldn't have been possible without wireless communication technologies such as Wi-Fi. In 1995 if you wanted to "surf" the Internet at home, you had to chain yourself to a network cable like it was an extension cord. In 1997, Wi-Fi was invented and released for consumer use. With a router and a dongle for our laptop, we could unplug from the network cable and roam the house or office and remain online.

Over the years, Wi-Fi's gotten progressively faster and found its way into computers, mobile devices and even cars. Wi-Fi is so essential to our personal and professional lives today that it's almost unheard of to be in a home or public place that doesn't have it.

BLUETOOTH

Another wireless communication technology that has proven indispensable is Bluetooth, a radio link that connects devices over short distances. Introduced to consumers in 1999, Bluetooth was built for connecting a mobile phone to a hands-free headset, allowing you to carry on conversations while keeping your hands available for other uses, such as driving a car.

Bluetooth has since expanded to link devices like earbuds, earphones, portable wireless speakers and hearing aids to audio sources like phones, PCs, stereo receivers and even cars. Fitness trackers use Bluetooth to stream data to mobile phones, and PCs can connect wirelessly to keyboards and mice.

Between 2012 and 2018, the number of Bluetooth-enabled devices in the world nearly tripled to ten billion (Poly, 2016). Today, Bluetooth is being employed in the smart home for uses such as unlocking doors and beaming audio to light bulbs with built-in speakers.

FACIAL RECOGNITION

Facial recognition is a blossoming field of technology that's playing an ever-growing role in our lives. It's a form of biometric authentication that uses the features of your face to verify your identity. The tech helps us unlock devices and sort photos in digital albums, but surveillance and marketing may end up being its prime uses. Cameras linked to facial recognition databases containing millions of mugshots and driver's license photos are used to identify suspected criminals. They also could be used to recognize your face and make personalized shopping recommendations as you enter a store.

ARTIFICIAL INTELLIGENCE

Artificial intelligence—simulating human intelligence in machines—used to be confined to science fiction. But in recent decades, it's broken into the real world, becoming one of the most important technologies of our time. In addition to being the brains behind facial recognition, AI is helping to solve critical problems in transportation, retail and health care. On the Internet, it's used for everything from speech recognition to spam filtering. But there's also fear that a dystopian future is looming with the creation of autonomous weapons, including drones, missile defense systems and sentry robots.

Did any items on this list capture your attention? All the technology can be overwhelming, but taken individually, it can all be very helpful. Use your creativity and think about just one of the items we looked at in this chapter and ask yourself how you could make it even better. When it comes to technology, there is always room for improvement.

In the next chapter, we will turn our focus to look at how engineering plays a huge part in the advances made in technology. Don't forget your pencil and notebook!

4

Electric Engineering

So far in our journey to learn about different jobs people do in and for technology, we've come across some pretty cool careers and inventions. Remember, the goal of this book is to get you thinking about your talents and how they might connect to one or more aspects of the tech world.

Hopefully you have your notebook open to a blank page. If not, why not grab one and dive into your awesome imagination? You'll be amazed at what you can create. And you never know what kind of sketch you make now could turn out to be the invention that revolutionizes the technology industry in the future.

Now let's meet some cutting-edge engineers who are creating truly amazing things in the world of technology!

MINJUAN ZHANG: THE ENGINEER MAKING CARS INVISIBLE

Minjuan and her team at Toyota are working to try to provide unobstructed views for car occupants of the future. To this end, they are attempting to build an "invisibility cloak" for future Toyotas (Zenco, 2018).

Zhang is a lifelong Toyota engineer and material scientist—she also holds at least fifty patents. Her main research focus is studying how light interacts with materials.

DOI: 10.4324/9781003263142-4

In 2016 her research yielded some interesting results that enabled her to develop a new paint color called "Structural Blue." By studying how light interacts with butterflies, the scientist invented the new paint that provided the unique deep blue color offered in the 2017 Lexus LC 500 series.

Zhang and her team are currently trying to find a way to render the internal structures of cars "invisible." The solution will involve the clever use of lenses and polarized light.

This technology is still very much a guarded secret kept by Toyota. If successful, it could become the standard for all modes of transportation.

CARMEL MAJIDI: THE ENGINEER HOPING TO MAKE SELF-HEALING MACHINES

Carmel Majidi is a Professor and Engineer at Carnegie Mellon University currently working on a method to allow machines to repair themselves like living organisms. Their material is able to repair itself once it has suffered severe mechanical damage!

The material is made from liquid metal droplets that are suspended within a soft elastomer. Once damaged, the droplets rupture like blood in an animal to form new connections with neighboring droplets to reroute electrical signals.

"Other research in soft electronics has resulted in materials that are elastic and deformable, but still vulnerable to mechanical damage that causes immediate electrical failure," explained Carmel. "The unprecedented level of functionality of our self-healing material can enable soft-matter electronics and machines to exhibit the extraordinary resilience of soft biological tissue and organisms" (Zenco, 2018).

ZHONG LIN WANG AND GEORGIA TECH ARE MAKING POWER GENERATING CLOTHS

Zhong Lin Wang, Professor in the Georgia Tech School of Materials Science and Engineering, is currently investigating the possibility of making a motion-generating energy harvesting material that clothes are made of. Not only that but their textile, once optimized, should also be bi-generational allowing it to harvest energy from solar generation. Motion-based electrical generation will be achieved using triboelectric nanogenerators. These work by combining triboelectric effects with electrostatic induction to generate electricity from any movement that agitates the textile.

The textile could have perfect applications as clothing but also in other fields that could take advantage of its bi-generational potential from wind and solar at the same time such as ships sails or energy harvesting flags. "This hybrid power textile presents a novel solution to charging devices in the field from something as simple as the wind blowing on a sunny day," explains Zhong Lin Wang (Zenco, 2018).

DAVID HANSON: THE ENGINEER BEHIND THE WORLD'S FIRST ROBOT CITIZEN

Dr. David Franklin Hanson Jr. is the man behind one of the most advanced AI androids ever built—Sophia. Activated in 2015 "she" was designed and built by his Hong Kong-based startup Hanson Robotics. Sophia made her debut at South by Southwest Festival in March of 2016 in Austin, Texas and has since become one of the most recognized robots of all time. Sophia is revolutionary in various ways but none more significant than "her" being awarded Saudi Arabian citizenship in 2017.

Sophia has since become a highly popular public speaker, especially for business, and has met face to face with many influential decision makers across many industries. She has also been named the first United Nations Innovation Champion by the United Nations Development Program (UNDP). In this position "she" will have an official role working with the UNDP to promote sustainable development and safeguard human rights and equality (Zenco, 2018).

Scan the QR code for a cool look at this amazing feat of robotics!

LUCIAN GHEORGHE: THE ENGINEER MERGING DRIVERS WITH CARS

Nissan and Dr. Lucian Gheorghe recently revealed their ambitions to allow drivers to communicate directly with their cars. They are working on a special piece of headgear that measures the wearer's brain waves.

The idea is for the car's autonomous systems to then analyze the information in real time with the view of anticipating the driver's future intentions. Dubbed Brain-to-Vehicle, B2V for short, they hope that the technology will be able to predict driver behavior and improve reaction times by 0.2 to 0.5 seconds! (Zenco, 2018)

CHUNYI ZHI: HELPING BUILD ELECTRICAL GENERATING YARN

A collaboration of engineers led by Chunyi Zhi from various Chinese Institutions (City University of Hong Kong, Shenzhen University, Harbin Institute of Technology, and the Graduate School at Shenzhen, Tsinghua University) are working together to develop a high-performance, waterproof, tailorable and stretchable yarn zinc ion battery (ZIB).

This battery is able to generate electricity whenever the fiber is stretched, bent, washed or cut. The battery is formed into a double-helix yarn of electrodes and a cross-linked polyacrylamide (PAM) electrolyte.

"We also have a plan to develop other types of yarn batteries with more functions such as self-healing ability, or self-charge capability when combined with a solar cell component," said Chunyi Zhi (Patel, 2018).

HUBERT WALTL AND AUDI ARE DESIGNING THE FACTORIES OF THE FUTURE

In 2017 Hubert Waltl and Audi released their plans for a model factory of the future—they called it their smart factory. This factory will make use of a number of new manufacturing technologies and, if successful, might reveal the future of all factories.

These new technologies include the use of 3D printers to build parts such as metal components, VR headsets for the design process and the use of drones to transport material around the facility. It is estimated that the new factory could improve productivity by as much as 20%. The new process will move away from production lines to a new concept of the modular assembly. This process will be tested at their engine plant in Győr, Hungary (Zenco, 2018).

DUONG HAI MINH IS MAKING AEROGEL FROM PAPER

Aerogels are widely considered to be the future of super-materials. They are used for so many everyday products like paint, makeup, firefighter suits and windows. They are strong like plastic but a lot lighter. A new method for making them from the cellulose fibers of recycled paper could also make the materials biodegradable.

These new biodegradable aerogels would be a lot cheaper and greener to make than "traditional" aerogels that require the use of silica gel and a specialized process. The new technique could make aerogels even more indispensable.

Duong Hai Minh and his team at the National University of Singapore managed to devise a surprisingly simple process to the make the new aerogels. It involves breaking down the paper into cellulose using water. A polymer resin is then added to form the material's shape and rigidity. The water is then extracted from the mixture using a high-frequency sound machine and then frozen for 24 hours.

Finally, it is air-dried and cured in an oven for three hours at 114 degrees Celsius. The final cellulose aerogel consists of 98.2% air while retaining its qualities as a flexible incredible insulator. It can also be made hydrophobic by adding a chemical coating (Zenco, 2018).

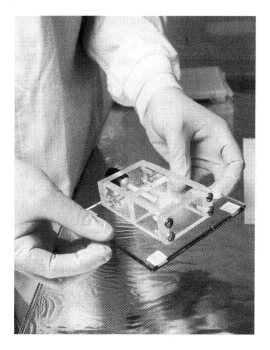

SETH GOLDSTEIN AND TODD MOWRY ARE CREATING PROGRAMMABLE MATTER

Claytronics is a project currently being undertaken by Seth Goldstein and Todd Mowry at Carnegie Mellon University. It is currently still considered an abstract future concept that will combine nanoscale robotics with computer science.

The idea is that individual nanometer computers, called claytronics (or Catoms), could interact with one another to create larger

3D objects. It falls under the banner term of programmable matter and it has the potential to greatly affect the world around us.

If it is ever realized, it could literally transform the world of telecommunications, human-computer interface and, of course, entertainment. In 2005, research had created mini scale cylindrical prototypes forty-four millimeters in diameter which were able to interact with each other via electromagnetic attraction.

Recent advancements in this prototype concept are in the form of one-millimeter diameter cylindrical robots fabricated on a thin film by photolithography. These micro-robots were able to cooperate with each other using complex software that would control electromagnetic attraction and repulsion between modules (Zenco, 2018).

SARA STABENOW: HELPING DEVELOP THE FUEL CELLS OF THE FUTURE

Sara Stabenow is helping GM develop fuel cell technology for the in-development SURUS (Silent Utility Rover Universal Superstructure) vehicle. The end result would be a flexible fuel cell electric platform that will have autonomous capabilities and is planned to be adapted for military use.

SURUS will use GM and Honda's Hydrotec Fuel Cell system. This tech, once perfected, should provide zero emission propulsion.

Sara holds a Bachelor's and Master's degree in Material Science and Engineering from Ohio State University. She worked for Honda's Research and Development America Inc. after graduating but later moved to GM (Zenco, 2018).

TIM COOK AND APPLE'S DAISY ARE PAVING THE WAY FOR THE FUTURE OF ELECTRONICS RECYCLING

Early this year Apple revealed their automated phone recycling robot called Daisy. This robot is able to disassemble as many as 200 iPhones an hour, from the iPhone5 to the iPhone7 Plus.

The process recovers the phones' main logic board, speaker, camera and other components containing high-quality materials. With rare earth metals slowly becoming scarcer this could be the perfect solution for Apple and other electronics manufacturers.

Apple currently has one unit in operation in Austin, Texas and plans to produce a second one in the Netherlands.

Apple users are encouraged to give their old iPhones to local Apple Stores for recycling through their GiveBack scheme. Some models are also eligible for the customer to receive credit that can be redeemed at Apple Stores on a gift card (Zenco, 2018).

ANASTASIOS JOHN HART AND HIS TEAM ARE HELPING LAMBORGHINI MAKE A SELF-HEALING CAR

Prof. Anastasios John Hart and Stefano Domenicali and other researchers at MIT have been collaborating with Lamborghini to develop their Terzo Millennio electric supercar. Apart from its use of a supercapacitor to replace a "standard" battery for power, the car will make use of carbon nanotubes for its bodywork.

The idea is to allow the car's bodywork to "heal" itself, mend fractures and correct other imperfections without human assistance. Although how this is actually achieved is a closely guarded secret, according to their sales material the car will be able to detect and repair cracks autonomously.

It will use sensors to monitor its own health and then fix any damage by filling it with nanotubes (Zenco, 2018).

RADHIKA NAGPAL: DEVELOPING ARTIFICIAL SWARM INTELLIGENCE

Swarm robotics or "artificial swarm intelligence" is a method for coordinating multiple simple physical robots. Like large colonies of insects, the robots will act in a desired collective behavior as they navigate their environment and communicate with one another.

In contrast to distributed robotic systems, swarm robotics places more emphasis on using a large number of drone robots and is a system that is hugely scalable. Research conducted by Radhika Nagpal and colleagues into this future technology is being undertaken in various institutions including at Harvard.

If it can be achieved, swarm robotics will have many cool uses from health care to military aid. As the drone robots are made smaller and smaller, it might be possible to coordinate nanoscale robot swarms to perform tasks in micro machinery or even in the human body.

They could also be used for mining and agricultural applications or find uses during rescue missions or disaster scenarios to access hard-to-reach places. More controversially, swarms of military robots may also form an autonomous army.

US Naval forces have tested a swarm of autonomous boats that can steer and take offensive actions by themselves. The boats are unmanned and can be fitted with a variety of kits to deter and destroy enemy vessels (Zenco, 2018).

MARC RAIBERT: THE ENGINEER BUILDING SELF-BALANCING ROBOTS

Marc Raibert and his team at Boston Dynamics have been in the news quite a lot lately with their suite of robots with almost animal-like abilities. From their canned US Military BigDog project to their Atlas heavy lifter robot and Wildcat drones, they are making real headway in robotics designs for the future. Most famous, of course, was the recently released footage of their uncannily agile acrobatic robot Handle.

Marc Raibert founded Boston Dynamics in 1992 after spending some time as an MIT Professor. Since then, the company has made huge developments in the design and creation of self-balancing robots. The company has changed hands a few times over the past few years. It was initially purchased for an undisclosed sum in 2013 by Google who then sold it off to SoftBank in 2017 (Zenco, 2018).

SKYLAR TIBBITS IS LEADING THE WAY TO DEVELOPING 4D PRINTING

Building on the breakthroughs made in 3D printing over the last decade or so, some researchers led by Skylar Tibbits at IT and Stratasys are working on adding another dimension to the process—time.

This future technology introduces a means of having any 3D printed material adapt over time after creation. It is, in a way, a special application of programmable matter but the printed material is able to react (with parameters) to a given environment or set of conditions.

This could provide near infinite configurations at the micrometer scale. 4D printing is fundamentally based in stereolithography, where, in most cases, ultraviolet light is used to cure the layered materials after the printing process has completed (Zenco, 2018).

Δ

These engineers are really coming up with cool inventions that build on the technology we already use. Did something in one of their stories interest you? It's hard to imagine that something as massive as Amazon didn't exist at one point. In that case, Jeff Bezos had an idea and made it happen. The same could be true for you!

Now let's take a look at how people use math to create all the cool tech gadgets we use.

5

Micro Math

Numbers are everywhere, and when it comes to technology the same holds true. Computers are, in many ways, calculators and logic machines with various input and output mechanisms. Statistics are used for basic research, which fuels the development of new technology.

The processors that power computers are able to perform calculations quickly, and the calculations are performed using Boolean algebra. People generally solve math problems using a base-10 number system. Boolean algebra relies on base-2 math, in which all numbers are represented using ones and zeros.

In addition to calculating basic math problems, however, computers also use Boolean logic. This logic allows computers to solve problems that require making logical decisions. Boolean algebra and logic combine to make sophisticated devices like self-driving cars, for example, which use the input calculated from digital cameras to make decisions about how to drive.

Modern technology depends on research to advance. GPS devices must know the speed of light to work, and this value is determined with math and experimentation using statistics. Advanced medical devices are supported by statistics. Even smartphones and tablet computers are only produced when surveys and other forms of customer feedback, which rely on math, predict that they are profitable.

DOI: 10.4324/9781003263142-5

ABACUS

The first technological leap dealt with rocks. In the beginning, people used small stones or other objects to count. The word *calculate* itself comes from the Latin *calculus*, which means *small stone*. Over time, people realized that this method did not go far enough to satisfy their increasing needs. To count up to 1,000, for example, they would have had to gather a thousand pebbles, which was enormous work.

Over time, the usual pebbles were replaced with stones of various sizes to which different orders of units were assigned. For example, if a decimal system was used, the number 1 could be represented by a small stone, 10 by a larger one, 100 by a still larger one, and so on. Do you remember the base-10 blocks your teacher used in elementary school? That's the same concept.

The counting board, or abacus, was invented when someone had the idea of placing pebbles or other objects in columns marked on a flat surface, and assigning an order of units to the objects in each column. Later, loose objects in columns were replaced with beads that could slide along parallel rods.

SLIDE RULE

The slide rule is basically a sliding stick that uses logarithmic scales to allow for fast multiplication and division. Slide rules evolved to allow advanced trigonometry and logarithms, exponentials and square roots. Even up to the 1980s, knowing how to operate a slide rule was a basic part of mathematics education for millions of schoolchildren, even though by that time mechanical and electric calculating machines were well established. The issue was that these weren't a fast solution to solving complex math problems.

CALCULATORS

The first mechanical calculator appeared way back in 1642! It was the creation of French math whiz Blaise Pascal and used geared wheels and could add and subtract two numbers directly and multiply and divide by repetition.

The Curta calculator, which first appeared in 1948, was perhaps the ultimate expression of the mechanical calculator, so compact that it could fit into a pocket and was capable of addition, subtraction, multiplication and division.

Machines like this ensured that mechanical calculators dominated twentieth century office life all the way through to the late 1960s.

THE ELECTRONIC AGE

In 1946, the construction of the ENIAC (Electronic Numerical Integrator And Computer) brought about a completely digital calculator capable of solving the four basic arithmetical functions. This machine was 1,000 times faster than electro-mechanical computers and could hold a ten-digit decimal number in memory (Swaine and Freiberger, 2022).

But to do this required 17,468 vacuum tubes, 7,200 crystal diodes, 1,500 relays, 70,000 resistors, 10,000 capacitors and around 5 million hand-soldered joints. It weighed around 27 tons, took up 1,800 square feet of floorspace and consumed as much power as a small town!

TRANSISTOR AGE

Transistors were the invention that replaced the fragile glass tubes used in previous counting machines. This new advance in technology allowed for lower costs and more efficient use of electricity to provide more computing power.

In 1967, a company called Texas Instruments released their landmark "Cal Tech" prototype, a calculator that could add, multiply, subtract and divide, and print results to a paper tape while being compact enough to be held in the hand. This device was extremely popular and relied on transistors to get the job done (Valentine, 2019).

COMPUTERS

The earliest electronic computers were enormous and expensive, and they required a team of engineers and other specialists to keep them running. One of the first and most famous of these, the Electronic Numerical Integrator Analyzer and Computer (ENIAC), cost $500,000, weighed 30 tons and took up nearly 2,000 square feet of floor space. On the outside, ENIAC was covered in cables, blinking lights and nearly 6,000 mechanical switches that its operators used to tell it what to do. On the inside, almost 18,000 vacuum tubes carried electrical signals from one part of the machine to another. The cool thing, however, was that ENIAC could solve in 30 seconds a math problem that would take a team of human "computers" 12 hours to complete! (Swaine and Freiberger, 2022)

One of the most significant inventions in technology that paved the way for the PC revolution was the microprocessor. Microprocessors were the size of a thumbnail, and they could do things the integrated-circuit chips could not: they could run the computer's programs, remember information and manage data all by themselves. The first microprocessor on the market was developed in 1971 by an engineer at Intel named Ted Hoff. Intel's first microprocessor had the same computing power as the massive ENIAC (History.com Editors, 2011).

THE INVENTION OF THE PC

In April 1975 two young programmers from Harvard formed a company of their own—Microsoft—that quickly became the empire it is today. The year after Gates and Allen started Microsoft, two engineers named Steve Jobs and Stephen Wozniak built a homemade computer that would likewise change the world called the Apple I. In April 1977, Jobs and Wozniak introduced the Apple II, which had a keyboard and a color screen. Also, users could store their data on an external cassette tape. (Apple soon swapped those tapes for floppy disks.) To make the Apple

II as useful as possible, the company encouraged programmers to create "applications" for it (History Computer Staff, 2021).

THE PC REVOLUTION

Soon, companies like Xerox, Tandy, Commodore and IBM had entered the market, and computers were in offices and eventually homes all over. Innovations like the "Graphical User Interface," which allows users to select icons on the computer screen instead of writing complicated commands, and the computer mouse made PCs even more convenient and user-friendly. Today, laptops, smartphones and tablet computers allow us to have a PC with us wherever we go.

Δ

From simple stones to powerful computers, math made a way for all of these technologies to exist. Along the way, brave men and women used their talents to figure out better, more effective ways of getting things done. That's where you come in. Think about all the technology you use and dream up ways you can make them better.

Scan the QR code for a cool review on how the technology of computers has changed over time.

 Take notes and diagrams as you watch the video in your notebook. You have the ability to come up with the next piece of technology that changes everything. Keep thinking. Dreaming. Creating. You're on your way to accomplishing big things!

6

Inside the HQs

How would you like to work in one of the coolest office buildings on Earth? If you go into the tech industry and get a job with either Apple or Google you might just get that opportunity. Let's take a break from the fact finding and go on a pretend tour of the two tech giants' massive headquarters.

APPLE HQ

Named "Apple Park," the new headquarters for Apple cost a staggering $5 billion! Built in Cupertino, California, Apple Park is built on 176 acres of land and took eight years to go through the planning, proposal, permit application, and construction processes. In 2017, the 12,000 Apple employees began working from the "spaceship," filling in the four-story, 2,800,000 square foot building (Apple Insider Staff, 2022).

Eco-Friendly
Apple co-founder Steve Jobs required that the campus be more like a nature refuge than an office park, so some eighty percent of Apple Park is green space that has been planted with drought-resistant trees and indigenous plants. Large orchards dot the property and supply fruit for the cafeterias. The roof is covered in solar panels, which provide approximately seventy-five percent

DOI: 10.4324/9781003263142-6

of the campus's power needs. The building is also designed to resist earthquakes.

The circular building is immense, measuring one mile in circumference—buses and bikes are provided for employees to get from one end of the campus to the other. Under the building is a network of roads and parking spaces. The campus also features seven cafes and a 100,000 square foot fitness center. The Steve Jobs Theater seats 1,000 people. There are also two large buildings for the research and development facilities as well as a care clinic for employees.

The Ring

Shaped like a large flying saucer of sorts, Apple calls the main campus building The Ring. This massive building features 800 forty-five-foot-tall rounded glass panels that connect all the way around the four-story structure. Some of these panels function as large sliding doors, allowing for the interior to be exposed to the outdoors during nice weather.

The Ring's interior hosts large rooms with glass walls and entryways, including wide-open spaces that can be collapsed into smaller sections as needed. The Ring is divided into eight identical segments and surrounded by a hallway roughly three-quarters of a mile around.

The Ring uses natural ventilation to aid in making it the greenest office building in the world, requiring no heating or cooling for nine months out of the year.

Steve Jobs Theater

The Steve Jobs Theater is a 165-foot diameter circular glass building without visible supports. The carbon-fiber roof is the largest in the world. Underneath the glass structure, underground, is an auditorium seating 1,000 people.

Visitors' Center

The Apple Park Visitor Center overlooks the campus and is divided into four sections: a 10,000-square-foot Apple Store, a 2,000-square-foot cafe, an observation deck, and an area for an AR experience. The augmented reality area is a scale model of

Apple Park that lets you view the campus via an iPad using AR software.

Glendenning Barn

The barn is a historical landmark moved and restored by Apple during Apple Park's construction. It was originally a part of the farmland that housed apricot, prune and cherry orchards. The barn is now used for simple storage of groundskeeping tools, but still stands as a symbol of community and innovation at Apple Park.

Scan the QR code to take a virtual tour of epic Apple Park! You might want to work there someday.

Apple Park is a wonder of architecture and technology. Now it's time to pretend that we're hopping in our car and driving five miles northwest to Mountain View, California, so we can check out Google's awesome headquarters!

GOOGLE HQ

Also called the Googleplex, the company's global headquarters has legendary perks including wellness classes, cafes, and office designs that will put the average cubicle to shame. The Googleplex added 31,276 square feet of themed amenity space that includes three cafes, a fitness center and seating areas in 2019. It's called Salt, based on the history of salt production in the area. The old ghost town of Saline City and its salt marshes were a source of salt production dating back to 1854.

The original complex has 2,000,000 square feet of office space. It is the company's second largest building. The Bay View addition to the building was added in 2015. This made it part of the biggest collection of Google buildings.

The buildings are not tall, but the complex covers a large area of land. The inside of the headquarters has items like shade lamps and giant rubber balls for decoration. The lobby has a piano and a projection of current live Google searches. There are also facilities like free laundry rooms, two small swimming pools, volleyball courts and eighteen cafeterias with different menus.

Finding your way around the Googleplex can be a little intimidating. Many of the employees at Google started work straight out of college. Their young age adds to the impression that you're on a college campus.

As soon as you walk into a Google lobby, you know you're not in a typical office environment as you watch lava lamps provide a groovy vibe.

Google advocates a green-conscious and healthy lifestyle among its employees, so it's not unusual to see bicycles parked in Google buildings. The offices don't resemble a typical corporate environment. Google arranges the workstations so that groups of three to four employees who work together sit in the same area.

Glass walls divide the space into clusters. This design cuts down on much of the ambient noise inside the office. It also allows sunlight to filter in through the entire office. Each glass enclosure has a tent-like roof made of acrylic-coated polyester which contains the room's lighting and sprinkler systems.

Google executives want employees to be able to bounce ideas off each other. It's the company's hope that by encouraging interaction, workers will have greater job satisfaction and may even create the next big Google product. Employees can personalize their workstations as much as they like, and even bring dogs (but not cats) to work if they want to.

Meal Time

Here's a neat fact: when you're hungry, your options range from vegetarian dishes to sushi to ethnic foods from around the world. Google's culture promotes the use of fresh, organic foods and healthy meals. But when everything is free and you can eat whenever you want, it's easy to go overboard. That's where the Google 15 comes in. It refers to the 15 pounds many new Google employees put on once they start taking advantage of all the meals and snacks.

Scan the QR code to get a wicked inside look at Google's massively tech-filled headquarters!

Δ

Both of these office complexes inspire the people who work at Google and Apple to use their creativity to come up with ideas and visions that will help the companies make inspiring products. Did you read something that grabbed hold of your attention? Of course, there are tons of other businesses with cool headquarters all over the world, although because of the Covid-19 pandemic many employees have been working from home.

Whatever path you take, landing a job in the technology industry will provide you with years of opportunities to shine. And who knows, maybe by the time you've graduated college, new companies with even more creative office buildings will be waiting for you to consider.

7

Who's Who?

Now let's take a brief look at some influential men and women in the tech industry and their backgrounds. There are tons of people who have done great things when it comes to technology. If we were talking about a Hall of Fame list of tech people, that list would include Steve Jobs, Bill Gates, Larry Page, Sergey Brin, Mark Zuckerberg, Jeff Bezos, Susan Wojcicki, Sheryl Sandberg, Ginni Rometty and Amy Hood.

STEVE JOBS

Jobs was born on February 24, 1955, in San Francisco, California. He lived with his adoptive family in Mountain View, California, within the area that would later become known as Silicon Valley. As a boy, Jobs and his father worked on electronics in the family garage. He showed his son how to take apart and reconstruct electronics, a hobby that Jobs loved.

Education and College

While Jobs was always an intelligent and innovative thinker, he didn't care for formal schooling. Jobs liked to play pranks in elementary school because he was bored, and it's said that his fourth-grade teacher needed to bribe him to study. Jobs test scores were so high, however, that administrators wanted to skip him ahead to high school—a proposal that his parents declined.

DOI: 10.4324/9781003263142-7

After high school, Jobs enrolled at Reed College in Portland, Oregon. Lacking direction, he dropped out of college after six months and spent the next eighteen months dropping in on creative classes at the school. In 1974, Jobs took a position as a video game designer with Atari.

Steve Wozniak and Steve Jobs

Back when Jobs was enrolled at Homestead High School, he was introduced to his future partner and co-founder of Apple Computers, Wozniak, who was attending the University of California, Berkeley.

In 1976, when Jobs was just twenty-one, he and Wozniak started Apple Computers in the Jobs' family garage. They funded their entrepreneurial venture by Jobs selling his Volkswagen bus and Wozniak selling his beloved scientific calculator.

Jobs and Wozniak revolutionized the computer industry with Apple by making machines smaller, cheaper, intuitive and accessible to everyday consumers.

Wozniak conceived of a series of user-friendly personal computers, and—with Jobs in charge of marketing—Apple initially marketed the computers for $666.66 each. The Apple I earned the corporation around $774,000. Three years after the release of Apple's second model, the Apple II, the company's sales increased by 700 percent to $139 million.

In 1980, Apple Computers became a publicly traded company, with a market value of $1.2 billion by the end of its very first day of trading. In 1984, Apple released the Macintosh, marketing the computer as a piece of a counterculture lifestyle: romantic, youthful, creative. But despite positive sales and performance superior to IBM's PCs, Apple still wasn't a competitor of IBM.

Fast forward to 2007. Steve Jobs announced the very first iPhone. The rest, they say, is history! (Biography.com Editors, 2022, *Steve Jobs*)

BILL GATES

Gates was born William Henry Gates III on October 28, 1955, in Seattle, Washington. Gates grew up in an upper-middle-class family with his older sister, Kristianne, and younger sister, Libby. Their father, William H. Gates Sr., was a promising, if somewhat shy, law student when he met his future wife, Mary Maxwell. She was an athletic, outgoing student at the University of Washington, actively involved in student affairs and leadership (Biography.com Editors, 2022, *Bill Gates*).

Education

Gates loved to read as a child, spending many hours poring over reference books such as the encyclopedia. Around the age of eleven or twelve, Gates's parents began to have concerns about his behavior. He was doing well in school, but he seemed bored and withdrawn at times, and his parents worried he might become a loner.

Though they were strong believers in public education, when Gates turned thirteen, his parents enrolled him at Seattle's exclusive preparatory Lakeside School. He blossomed in nearly all his subjects, excelling in math and science, but also doing very well in drama and English. While at Lakeside, a Seattle computer company offered to provide computer time for the students.

The Mother's Club used proceeds from the school's rummage sale to purchase a teletype terminal for students to use. Gates became entranced with what a computer could do and spent much of his free time working on the terminal. He wrote a tic-tac-toe program in BASIC computer language that allowed users to play against the computer.

Gates graduated from Lakeside in 1973. He scored 1590 out of 1600 on the college SAT test, a feat of intellectual achievement that he boasted about for several years when introducing himself to new people.

Harvard Dropout

Gates enrolled at Harvard University in the fall of 1973, originally thinking of a career in law. Much to his parents' dismay, Gates dropped out of college in 1975 to pursue his business, Microsoft, with his partner Allen. Gates had spent more of his time in the computer lab than in class. He had not really had a study regimen, and had got by on a few hours of sleep a day, cramming for tests and passing with a reasonable grade.

Meeting and Partnering with Paul Allen

Gates met Allen, who was two years his senior, in high school at Lakeside School. The pair became fast friends, bonding over their common enthusiasm for computers, even though they were very different people. Allen was more reserved and shy. Gates was feisty and at times hard to get along with.

Regardless of their differences, Allen and Gates spent much of their free time together working on programs. Occasionally, the two disagreed and would clash over who was right or who should run the computer lab. On one occasion, their argument escalated to the point where Allen banned Gates from the computer lab.

At one point, Gates and Allen had their school computer privileges revoked for taking advantage of software glitches to obtain free computer time from the company that provided the computers. After their probation, they were allowed back in the computer lab when they offered to debug the program. During this time, Gates developed a payroll program for the computer company the boys had hacked into and a scheduling program for the school.

In 1970, at the age of 15, Gates and Allen went into business together, developing "Traf-o-Data," a computer program that monitored traffic patterns in Seattle. They netted $20,000 for their efforts. Gates and Allen wanted to start their own company, but Gates' parents wanted him to finish school and go on to college, where they hoped he would work to become a lawyer.

Allen went to Washington State University, while Gates went to Harvard, though the pair stayed in touch. After attending college for two years, Allen dropped out and moved to Boston, Massachusetts, to work for Honeywell. Around this time, he showed Gates an edition of *Popular Electronics* magazine featuring an article on the Altair 8800 mini-computer kit. Both young men were fascinated with the possibilities of what this computer could create in the world of personal computing.

The Altair was made by a small company in Albuquerque, New Mexico, called Micro Instrumentation and Telemetry Systems (MITS). Gates and Allen contacted the company, proclaiming that they were working on a BASIC software program that would run the Altair computer. In reality, they didn't have an

Altair to work with or the code to run it, but they wanted to know if MITS was interested in someone developing such software.

MITS was, and its President, Ed Roberts, asked the boys for a demonstration. Gates and Allen scrambled, spending the next two months writing the BASIC software at Harvard's computer lab. Allen traveled to Albuquerque for a test run at MITS, never having tried it out on an Altair computer. It worked perfectly. Allen was hired at MITS, and Gates soon left Harvard to work with him. Together they founded Microsoft.

Allen remained with Microsoft until 1983, when he was diagnosed with Hodgkin's disease. Though his cancer went into remission a year later with intensive treatment, Allen resigned from the company.

Founding Microsoft

In 1975, Gates and Allen formed Micro-Soft, a blend of "micro-computer" and "software" (they dropped the hyphen within a year). The company's first product was BASIC software that ran on the Altair computer.

Another huge addition Gates and Microsoft made to the computer world was their introduction of Windows 1.0 back in 1985. Windows was revolutionary because it was a graphical user interface which allowed people to navigate their PCs with ease. Instead of typing in commands to access files, users could navigate around with a click of the mouse.

LARRY PAGE

Lawrence Page was born on March 26, 1973, in East Lansing, Michigan. His father, Carl Page, was a pioneer in computer science and artificial intelligence, and his mother taught computer programming. After earning a Bachelor of Science degree in engineering from the University of Michigan, Page decided to concentrate on computer engineering for graduate school at Stanford University, where he met Brin (Biography.com Editors, 2022, *Larry Page*).

Creating Google with Sergey Brin

As a research project at Stanford University, Page and Brin created a search engine that listed results according to the popularity of the pages, after concluding that the most popular result would often be the most useful. They called the search engine "Google" after the mathematical term "googol," which refers to the number 1 followed by 100 zeros, to reflect their mission to organize the immense amount of information available on the web.

After raising $1 million from family, friends and other investors, the pair launched the company in 1998. Google has since become the world's most popular search engine, receiving an average of 5.9 billion searches per day in 2013. Headquartered in the heart of California's Silicon Valley, Google held its initial public offering in August 2004, making Page and Brin billionaires.

On the Move

In 2006, Google purchased the most popular website for user-submitted streaming videos, YouTube, for $1.65 billion in stock.

In September 2013, Page was ranked No. 13 on the *Forbes* 400 list of the richest people in America. That October, he was ranked No. 17 on *Forbes'* 2013 "Most Powerful People" list. As Google's CEO, Page shared responsibility for the company's operations with Brin, who served as Director of Special Projects for Google, and Eric Schmidt, the company's Executive Chairman.

SERGEY BRIN

Sergey Brin is a computer scientist and entrepreneur. He met Larry Page at Stanford University, and the two created a search engine that would sort web pages based on popularity. Google became the most popular search engine in the world after launching in 1998, its overwhelming success turning the co-founders into billionaires. Brin and Page later became President and CEO of Google's parent company, Alphabet, before they stepped down from their roles in December 2019 (Biography.com Editors, 2022, *Sergey Brin*).

Early Life

Sergey Mikhaylovich Brin was born on August 21, 1973, in Moscow, Russia. The son of a Soviet mathematician and economist, Brin and his family emigrated to the United States to escape Jewish persecution in 1979. After receiving his degree in mathematics and computer science from the University of Maryland at College Park, Brin entered Stanford University, where he met Larry Page. Both students were completing doctorates in computer science.

The Beginning of Google

As a research project at Stanford University, Brin and Page created a search engine that listed results according to the popularity of the pages, after concluding that the most popular result would often be the most useful.

After raising $1 million from family, friends and other investors, the pair launched the company in 1998. Headquartered in the heart of California's Silicon Valley, today Google receives billions of searches worldwide per day.

Success, Technology and Expansion

In 2006, Google purchased the most popular website for user-submitted streaming videos, YouTube, for $1.65 billion in stock. Their tech acquisitions didn't stop there. In 2007, Google bought Waze, the popular GPS navigation software, as well as Fitbit, the popular consumer electronics devices. In 2012, Google bought telecommunications company Motorola and in 2014 they expanded their tech empire and bought Nest, the home automation technology, for three billion dollars. These are just a few of the major companies Google has purchased since the early 2000s. Maybe one day you will create some cool gadget of your own that Google is interested in buying. You never know, so dream big!

MARK ZUCKERBERG

Zuckerberg was born on May 14, 1984, in White Plains, New York, into a comfortable, well-educated family. He was raised in the nearby village of Dobbs Ferry.

Zuckerberg's father, Edward Zuckerberg, ran a dental practice attached to the family home. His mother, Karen, worked as a psychiatrist before the birth of the couple's four children—Mark, Randi, Donna and Arielle.

Zuckerberg developed an interest in computers at an early age; when he was about 12, he used Atari BASIC to create a messaging program he named "Zucknet." His father used the program in his dental office, so that the receptionist could inform him of a new patient without yelling across the room. The family also used Zucknet to communicate within the house.

Together with his friends, he also created computer games just for fun. "I had a bunch of friends who were artists," he said. "They'd come over, draw stuff, and I'd build a game out of it."

Education

To keep up with Zuckerberg's growing interest in computers, his parents hired private computer tutor David Newman to come to the house once a week and work with Zuckerberg. Newman later told reporters that it was hard to stay ahead of the prodigy, who began taking graduate courses at nearby Mercy College around this same time.

Zuckerberg later studied at Phillips Exeter Academy, an exclusive preparatory school in New Hampshire. There he showed talent in fencing, becoming the captain of the school team. He also excelled in literature, earning a diploma in classics.

Yet Zuckerberg remained fascinated by computers and continued to work on developing new programs. While still in high school, he created an early version of the music software Pandora, which he called Synapse (Biography.com Editors, 2022, *Mark Zuckerberg*).

Several companies—including AOL and Microsoft—expressed an interest in buying the software, and hiring the teenager before graduation. He declined the offers.

College Experience

After graduating from Exeter in 2002, Zuckerberg enrolled at Harvard University.

By his sophomore year, he had a reputation as the go-to software developer on campus. It was at that time that he built a program called CourseMatch, which helped students choose their classes based on the course selections of other users.

He also invented Facemash, which compared the pictures of two students on campus and allowed users to vote on which one was more attractive. The program became wildly popular, but was later shut down by the school administration after it was deemed inappropriate.

Based on the buzz of his previous projects, three of his fellow students—Divya Narendra, and twins Cameron and Tyler Winklevoss—sought him out to work on an idea for a social networking site they called Harvard Connection. This site was designed to use information from Harvard's student networks in order to create a dating site for the Harvard elite.

Zuckerberg agreed to help with the project, but soon dropped out to work on his own social networking site, The Facebook. After his sophomore year, Zuckerberg dropped out of college to devote himself to his new company, Facebook, full time.

Founding Facebook

Zuckerberg and his friends Dustin Moskovitz, Chris Hughes and Eduardo Saverin created The Facebook, a site that allowed users to create their own profiles, upload photos, and communicate with other users. The group ran the site out of a dorm room at Harvard University until June 2004.

That year Zuckerberg dropped out of college and moved the company to Palo Alto, California. By the end of 2004, Facebook had 1 million users.

In 2005, Zuckerberg's enterprise received a huge boost from the venture capital firm Accel Partners. Accel invested $12.7 million into the network, which at the time was open only to Ivy League students (Biography.com Editors, 2022, *Mark Zuckerberg*).

Zuckerberg's company then granted access to other colleges, high school and international schools, pushing the site's membership to more than 5.5 million users by December 2005. The site began attracting the interest of other companies that wanted to advertise with the popular social hub.

Not wanting to sell the business, Zuckerberg turned down offers from companies such as Yahoo! and MTV Networks. Instead, he focused on expanding the site, opening up his project to outside developers and adding more features. Today, Facebook has billions of users.

JEFF BEZOS

Bezos was born on January 12, 1964, in Albuquerque, New Mexico, to a teenage mother, Jacklyn Gise Jorgensen, and his biological father, Ted Jorgensen.

The Jorgensens were married less than a year. When Bezos was four years old, his mother remarried, to Mike Bezos, a Cuban immigrant.

Bezos showed an early interest in how things work, turning his parents' garage into a laboratory and rigging electrical contraptions around his house as a child.

He moved to Miami with his family as a teenager, where he developed a love for computers and graduated valedictorian of his high school. It was during high school that he started his first business, the Dream Institute, an educational summer camp for fourth, fifth and sixth graders.

Bezos graduated summa cum laude from Princeton University in 1986 with a degree in computer science and electrical engineering (Biography.com Editors, 2022, *Jeff Bezos*).

Career in Finance

After graduating from Princeton, Bezos found work at several firms on Wall Street, including Fitel, Bankers Trust and the investment firm D.E. Shaw. In 1990, Bezos became D.E. Shaw's youngest vice president.

While his career in finance was extremely lucrative, Bezos chose to make a risky move into the nascent world of e-commerce. He quit his job in 1994, moved to Seattle and targeted the untapped potential of the Internet market by opening an online bookstore.

Founder and CEO of Amazon.com

Bezos opened Amazon.com, named after the meandering South American river, on July 16, 1995, after asking 300 friends to beta test his site. In the months leading up to launch, a few employees began developing software with Bezos in his garage; they eventually expanded operations into a two-bedroom house equipped with three Sun Microstations.

The initial success of the company was meteoric. With no press promotion, Amazon.com had sold books across the United States and in 45 foreign countries within 30 days. In two months, sales reached $20,000 a week, growing faster than Bezos and his startup team had envisioned.

Amazon.com went public in 1997, leading many market analysts to question whether the company could hold its own when traditional retailers launched their own e-commerce sites. Two years later, the startup had not only kept up, but also outpaced competitors, becoming an e-commerce leader.

Bezos soon changed Amazon's offerings with the sale of CDs and videos in 1998, and later clothes, electronics, toys and more through major retail partnerships. Amazon flourished with yearly sales that jumped from $510,000 in 1995 to over $17 billion in 2011. By September 2018, Amazon was valued at more than $1 trillion, the second company to ever hit that record just a few weeks after Apple (Biography.com Editors, 2022, *Jeff Bezos*).

Kindle E-Reader

Amazon released the Kindle, a handheld digital book reader that allowed users to buy, download, read and store their book selections, in 2007.

SUSAN WOJCICKI

Susan Wojcicki is an American tech industry executive who is the CEO (2014–) of the video-sharing website YouTube. She previously was the Senior Vice President of Marketing at YouTube's parent company, Google Inc.

Wojcicki's father was a physics professor at Stanford University, and her mother was a teacher. She grew up in the Stanford, California, area and later studied history and literature at Harvard University (BA, 1990), economics at the University of California, Santa Cruz (MS, 1993), and business at the University of California, Los Angeles (MBA, 1998). After returning to Silicon Valley in 1998, she rented out garage space in her Menlo Park home to the newly incorporated Google Inc., which briefly used it as the company's first headquarters.

Google had moved to more conventional office space by the time Wojcicki went to work for the company in 1999. Her task as Google's first marketing manager was to find ways of generating revenue from the company's signature search engine. Her first big success came in 2000, with the debut of AdWords, the clickable text-only advertisements that appear on Google search pages.

Several of Wojcicki's subsequent successes at Google came from the purchase and nurturance of startup companies in the field of Internet advertising. With the launch of the AdSense system and the acquisition of Applied Semantics, both in 2003, Google became a broker of online display advertising. For a fee, the AdSense system placed appropriate advertisements on participating websites. When an advertisement was viewed or clicked on and agreed-upon conditions were met, the web publisher received some of the money that the advertiser had paid to Google.

Wojcicki's responsibilities greatly increased in 2008 with Google's acquisition of the company DoubleClick. Among other capabilities, the DoubleClick system deployed cookies that tracked the preferences of Internet users for the benefit of advertisers. Google kept pace with the rapid proliferation of smartphones when Wojcicki arranged for the purchase of the mobile advertising network AdMob in 2009.

Wojcicki first became involved with video sharing in connection with the launch of Google Video in 2005. The following year she oversaw the purchase of rival YouTube, an equally new venture that was enjoying greater success. The YouTube brand name was retained even after the company became a Google subsidiary. Wojcicki, who was elevated to Senior Vice President at Google in 2010, moved over to YouTube in 2014 and became the company's CEO later that year. She thus became head of an operation that claimed to have more than one billion monthly users (Biography.com Editors, 2022, *Susan Wojcicki*).

SHERYL SANDBERG

Sheryl Sandberg is Chief Operating Officer at Facebook, overseeing the firm's business operations. Her net worth is over a billion dollars. Prior to Facebook, Sheryl was Vice President of Global Online Sales and Operations at Google, Chief of Staff for the United States Treasury Department under President Clinton, a management consultant with McKinsey & Company and an economist with the World Bank. Sheryl received a BA summa cum laude from Harvard University and an MBA with highest distinction from Harvard Business School.

Sheryl is the co-author of *Option B: Facing Adversity, Building Resilience, and Finding Joy* with Wharton professor and bestselling author Adam Grant. She is also the author of the bestsellers *Lean In: Women, Work, and the Will to Lead* and *Lean In for Graduates*.

She is the founder of the Sheryl Sandberg & Dave Goldberg Family Foundation, a nonprofit organization that works to build a more equal and resilient world through two key initiatives, LeanIn.org and OptionB.org. Sheryl serves on the boards of Facebook, the Walt Disney Company, Women for Women International, ONE and SurveyMonkey. Sheryl lives in Menlo Park with her son and daughter (Biography.com Editors, 2022, *Sheryl Sandberg*).

GINNI ROMETTY

Ginni became CEO of IBM in 2012 and retired form the company on December 31, 2020. During her tenure she made bold changes to help IBM be ready for the future, investing in high-value segments of the IT market and optimizing the company's portfolio.

Under Ginni's leadership, IBM built out key capabilities in hybrid cloud, security, quantum computing, industry expertise, and data and AI, both organically and through acquisition. IBM acquired 65 companies during Ginni's tenure as CEO, including Red Hat, the largest acquisition in the company's history. She reinvented more than fifty percent of IBM's portfolio, built a $21 billion hybrid cloud business and established IBM's leadership in AI, quantum computing and blockchain technologies.

Ginni also established IBM as the model of responsible stewardship in the digital age. She was the industry's leading voice on technology ethics and data stewardship, working relentlessly to safely usher new technologies into society. She enabled people of diverse backgrounds and education levels to participate in the digital economy by building talent, skills and opportunity for disadvantaged populations (Biography.com Editors, 2022, *Ginni Rometty*).

Because of her leadership, IBM created thousands of New Collar jobs and championed the reinvention of education around the world, including the explosive growth of the six-year Pathways in Technology Early College High Schools, or P-TECHs, which are helping prepare the workforce of the future, serving hundreds of thousands of students in over 240 schools and 28 countries.

She also helped to redefine the purpose of the corporation through her work with the Business Roundtable, expanding corporate commitments to include a wide range of stakeholders, from customers to communities.

IBM also achieved record results in diversity and inclusion under Ginni's leadership. This included extending parental leave and making it easier for women to return to the workforce through a "returnships" program with hands-on work experience in emerging technologies. This pioneering work was recognized in 2018 by the prestigious Catalyst Award for advancing diversity and women's initiatives. IBM is the only tech company to have earned this recognition in the past 20 years and the only company ever to be honored four times.

Beginning her career with IBM in 1981, Ginni held a series of leadership positions across the company and led the successful integration of PricewaterhouseCoopers Consulting, creating a global team of more than 100,000 business consultants and services experts. Creating teams with diverse backgrounds will help make a business successful.

Ginni is also the Co-Chair of OneTen, a group that combines the power of committed US companies to upskill, hire and promote one million Black Americans over the next ten years into family-sustaining jobs with opportunities for advancement. She also serves on the Board of Directors of JPMorgan Chase, the Board of Trustees of Northwestern University, where she is a Vice Chair, the Board of Trustees of Memorial Sloan-Kettering Cancer Center, the Board of Trustees of the Brookings Institute, and the Council on Foreign Relations. Being a crucial part of all these teams ensures that Ginni's vision and heart are used to help many people who might otherwise not have the chance to see their dreams come true.

She has a Bachelor of Science degree with high honors in Computer Science and Electrical Engineering from Northwestern University, where she later was awarded an honorary degree. She also has honorary degrees from Rensselaer Polytechnic Institute and North Carolina State University.

AMY HOOD

Amy Hood is the Executive Vice President and Chief Financial Officer at Microsoft and is responsible for leading the company's worldwide finance organization, including business operations, acquisitions, treasury, tax planning, global real estate, accounting and reporting, internal audit and investor relations (Microsoft, 2022).

Hood joined Microsoft in 2002, and through her tenure with the company has advanced momentum in cloud computing and helped digitally transform the company. She is deeply involved in the company's operations, as well as the strategy development and overall execution of the company's successful acquisitions of LinkedIn and GitHub.

For the past eight years, she has acted as a strategic partner to Microsoft CEO Satya Nadella, propelling long-term financial growth, championing culture and driving corporate initiatives including Microsoft's climate and affordable housing commitments. She has also served on the Board of Directors of 3M since 2017.

Hood earned a Bachelor's degree in Economics from Duke University and a Master's degree in Business Administration from Harvard University.

YOU

These famous people are only a small handful of men and women who dedicated their lives to studying space in one way or another. Did one of them stand out to you? Why? You, too, can achieve the same goals if you work hard to develop your talents. The common thread through all of these people's stories is that they didn't quit. They figured out a way to build a team made of strong individuals who cared about helping others.

In the next chapter we will take a look at some cool job opportunities you may have when you graduate college.

8

A Motherboard of Opportunities

Technology seems to change daily. The latest versions of phones and computers aren't out for very long before the next round of devices are made available. Jobs for these products will never go away, but there are so many more areas of the tech world for you to consider!

PRODUCT MANAGER

One of the highest paying tech jobs, a product manager helps lead the development of tech products from conception to launch. Product managers have to have strong analytical and time management skills. They are responsible for not only making sure the product is built but also for the marketing and sales of it. The average yearly salary of a product manager is over $100,000.

ARTIFICIAL INTELLIGENCE (AI) ARCHITECT

An AI architect develops, manages and oversees AI initiatives within an organization. An AI architect should have strong knowledge of mathematics and statistics. AI architects have good programming skills and know Python, R and Torch, understand how TensorFlow and other similar technologies work,

DOI: 10.4324/9781003263142-8

and have a clear understanding about technologies related to AI, including machine learning, neural networks and deep learning. It's okay if you've never heard of any of these terms before. If this is an area of the tech industry that interests you, put a sticky note here and refer back as you get older. AI architects also earn over $100,000 a year for their work.

Scan the QR code to watch a fun video that explains how AI works!

FULL-STACK DEVELOPER

This is one of the highest-paid IT jobs in the industry. This job is called "full-stack" because this developer works on both sides of the application. They have to know all there is to know about servers (back end) as well as be able to help the users (front end). Here are some of the skills a pro full-stack developer has:

♦ Knowledge of technologies such as MongoDB, Express. js, AngularJS, and Node.js
♦ How to design and develop an API (application programming interface)
♦ Coding and scripting
♦ The fundamentals of web development
♦ Basics of database technologies

The average yearly salary of a full-stack developer comes in around $106,000.

CLOUD ARCHITECT

Next in the list of best paying jobs in technology is cloud architect. The "cloud" refers to software and services that run on the Internet instead of your local computer. A cloud architect creates and oversees an organization's cloud computing strategy.

Some of the skills and knowledge required by a cloud architect include:

- ◆ A thorough understanding of cloud application architecture
- ◆ Knowledge of Amazon Web Services (AWS), Azure or Google cloud platform
- ◆ Good communication skills

The average yearly salary of a cloud architect is $107,000.

DEVOPS ENGINEER

Next in the list of best paying jobs in technology is a DevOps engineer. This could refer to someone on the development team taking part in the deployment and network operations, or to someone from the operations team working on application development.

Some of the skills required of a DevOps engineer include coding and scripting, tools like Git and Jenkins, and knowledge of Linux or Unix operating systems. The average yearly salary of a DevOps engineer ranges from $95,000 to $140,000.

BLOCKCHAIN ENGINEER

Blockchain technology might be something you're not familiar with, but it is an area in high demand. A blockchain engineer specializes in developing and implementing architecture and solutions using blockchain technology. If you've ever created a Google Doc, you've experienced blockchain technology. When you share the document with your friend across town, he or she can see the changes you're making in real time. They don't have to wait for you to keep sharing the document.

Blockchain is used a lot in the cryptocurrency world with currencies like Bitcoin and Ethereum. A blockchain engineer should have solid programming skills and a thorough understanding of the technologies behind Ripple, R3, Ethereum and Bitcoin as well as consensus methodologies and the security protocol stacks, crypto libraries and functions. That sounds like a ton of things to be responsible for, but the average yearly salary of a blockchain engineer is well over $150,000! (Mazer, 2022)

SOFTWARE ARCHITECT

A software architect optimizes the development process by making design choices and dictating technical standards such as coding, tools and platforms. As part of their role, they identify a customer's requirements and perform hands-on work to develop prototypes. Some of the skills required of a software architect include:

♦ Data modeling
♦ An understanding of software architecture
♦ Good programming skills
♦ Strong analytical skills

The average yearly salary of a software architect is over $114,000.

BIG DATA ENGINEER

Internet users generate about 2.5 quintillion bytes of data each day! A quintillion is a "1" followed by eighteen zeroes! To harness and gain insights from such a huge amount of data, over 97 percent of organizations are investing in Big Data and AI.

A Big Data engineer plans, designs and manages the entire lifecycle of large-scale developments and deployments of Big Data applications. Some of the skills required of a Big Data architect include:

♦ Understanding Hadoop, Spark and NoSQL, as well as data warehousing technologies
♦ Programming skills
♦ Data visualization skills
♦ Excellent communication skills

The average yearly salary of a Big Data architect is $140,000.

IOT SOLUTIONS ARCHITECT

One of the most-in demand and best paying jobs in technology today is an IoT (Internet of Things) solutions architect. The IoT solutions architect is a leadership role of overseeing the strategy behind the development and deployment of IoT solutions. In addition to understanding IoT solutions, one should also have strong programming skills, an understanding of machine learning, and knowledge of hardware design and architecture.

An IoT solutions architect looks at all aspects of a company's technology to see how it can function best in the marketplace. IoTs can earn an average of over $130,000 annually.

DATA SCIENTIST

Data scientists have the highest paying jobs across the tech industry. A data scientist analyzes and interprets complex data to help organizations make better and more timely decisions. A data scientist should be able to:

- ◆ Understand machine learning algorithms
- ◆ Create data models
- ◆ Code in languages like Python, R and SAS and use other analytical tools
- ◆ Identify business issues and provide appropriate solutions

The yearly salary of a data scientist can be as high as $150,000.

9

But Wait, There's More!

We've covered so much information on technology your head might be spinning right about now. The goal of this chapter is to give you some other things to think about. We're going to look at some cool new and whacky gadgets in the tech world and hopefully inspire an even bigger interest for you in investigating some of them when you grow up.

As you go, don't forget about your notebook where you've been organizing your thoughts and see if you can come up with a list of your top three favorite concepts that we've investigated. That way you will be able to focus your energy for our last chapter that deals with what you can take in high school and what degree plans colleges offer in regard to specific technology careers.

Who knows, after all is said and done you might create your own career path!

Amazon Astro Household Robot
Astro is an anthropomorphized (has human characteristics) household assistant that can move freely around your home to keep an eye on things. Treat it like a pet or use it as a security drone, the choice is up to you. Hopefully, it's a sign that more household robots will soon be available to the average person.

Sonos Roam Smart Speaker
The Sonos Roam is a hybrid speaker that offers the best of both worlds with minimal compromise. When connected to a Wi-Fi

DOI: 10.4324/9781003263142-9

network, the Roam can take advantage of better audio quality and voice-controlled integration with Google Assistant and Alexa. When connected to your phone via Bluetooth, you can take the Roam wherever you want and have access to audio as long as your phone battery and the speaker's battery aren't dead.

Apple AirPods Max

These headphones are built with 3D surround sound that adjusts based on your environment and head position, and they've got active noise cancellation that blocks out the rest of the world with the press of a button. The headphones themselves have a knit-mesh canopy and memory foam ear cushions for a great fit. They're also built to seamlessly switch between devices, and have on-head detection so your music will pause if you need to remove them for a second!

Nook Casa Smart Light Bulbs

This smart light bulb costs $23 and is worth the price. Once you plug in and set up this bulb, you can literally choose from thousands of colors and bring mood lighting to any space.

Razer Kishi Gaming Controller

This innovative controller is one of the coolest tech gadgets from 2021 for mobile gamers. Smartphones are capable of playing some great games these days, and the Razer Kishi lets you snap the controller onto both ends of your device, mimicking the design of traditional video game controllers. This gives you the precision, control and full array of buttons you need to beat your competition.

Apple Watch Series 7

As of October 15, 2021, Apple has officially moved on to the Apple Watch Series 7, which carries over the Series 6's best features and ups the ante even more. The main improvement is to the Always-On retina display, which now has 20% more screen area than its predecessor.

According to Apple, the new Apple Watch is "the most durable Apple Watch ever, with a stronger, more crack-resistant front crystal. It is the first Apple Watch to have an IP6X certification for resistance to dust and maintains a WR50 water resistance rating" (Apple.com Editors, 2021).

Apple iPad Air

We still think it's kind of insane that Apple took many of the best aspects of its iPad Pro—namely the slim-bezel design and compatibility with the Magic Keyboard—dropped them into the newest iPad Air and offered it at a very reasonable price. As a result, for less than $600, you get a device that lets you stream Netflix and Spotify, FaceTime with your friends, doodle, draw and design with the Apple Pencil, and even use it like a traditional laptop. Even if tablets are not completely essential in most people's day-to-day lives like phones are, it's undeniable that an iPad is deeply pleasurable to use.

Oculus Quest 2

Virtual reality might be taking its time to have its "iPhone moment," but it is still very much the next big thing when it comes to the coolest tech gadgets. And there is not a single VR device that flashes that promise more than the Oculus Quest 2. Without the need for a powerful computer or special equipment, you can simply strap the Quest 2 to your head, pick up the controllers and move freely in VR space thanks to its inside out technology, which uses cameras on the outside of the headset to track your movement in the space around you.

THE FUTURE IS HERE

Lab-Made Dairy

You've heard of cultured "meat" and Wagyu steaks grown cell by cell in a laboratory, but what about other animal-based foodstuffs? A growing number of biotech companies around the world are investigating lab-made dairy, including milk, ice-cream, cheese and eggs. And more than one think they've cracked it (Science-Focus.com Editors, 2022).

The dairy industry is not environmentally friendly, not even close. It's responsible for four percent of the world's carbon emissions, more than air travel and shipping combined, and demand is growing for a greener splash to pour into our teacups and cereal bowls.

Compared with meat, milk isn't actually that difficult to create in a lab. Rather than grow it from stem cells, most researchers attempt to produce it in a process of fermentation, looking to produce the milk proteins whey and casein. Some products are already at market in the US, from companies such as Perfect Day, with ongoing work focused on reproducing the mouthfeel and nutritional benefits of regular cow's milk.

Bionic Eyes

Bionic eyes have been a mainstay of science fiction for decades, but now real-world research is beginning to catch up with far-sighted storytellers. A raft of technologies is coming to market that restore sight to people with different kinds of vision impairment.

In January 2021, Israeli surgeons implanted the world's first artificial cornea into a bilaterally blind, 78-year-old man. When his bandages were removed, the patient could read and recognize family members immediately. The implant also fuses naturally to human tissue without the recipient's body rejecting it (ScienceFocus.com Editors, 2022).

Likewise, in 2020 Belgian scientists developed an artificial iris fitted to smart contact lenses that correct a number of vision disorders. And scientists are even working on wireless brain implants that bypass the eyes altogether.

Researchers at Montash University in Australia are working on trials for a system whereby users wear a pair of glasses fitted with a camera. This sends data directly to the implant, which sits on the surface of the brain and gives the user a rudimentary sense of sight.

Energy Bricks

Scientists have found a way to store energy in the red bricks that are used to build houses.

Researchers led by Washington University in St Louis, in Missouri, US, have developed a method that can turn the cheap and widely available building material into "smart bricks" that can store energy like a battery (ScienceFocus.com Editors, 2022).

Although the research is still in the proof-of-concept stage, the scientists claim that walls made of these bricks "could store a substantial amount of energy" and can "be recharged hundreds of thousands of times within an hour."

The researchers developed a method to convert red bricks into a type of energy storage device called a supercapacitor. This involved putting a conducting coating, known as Pedot, onto brick samples, which then seeped through the fired bricks' porous structure, converting them into "energy storing electrodes."

Sweat-Powered Watches

Engineers at the University of Glasgow have developed a new type of flexible supercapacitor which stores energy by replacing the electrolytes found in conventional batteries with sweat.

It can be fully charged with as little as twenty microlitres of fluid and is robust enough to survive 4,000 cycles of the types of flexes and bends it might encounter in use.

The device works by coating polyester cellulose cloth in a thin layer of a polymer which acts as the supercapacitor's electrode. As the cloth absorbs its wearer's sweat, the positive and negative ions in the sweat interact with the polymer's surface, creating an electrochemical reaction which generates energy.

"Conventional batteries are cheaper and more plentiful than ever before but they are often built using unsustainable materials which are harmful to the environment," says Professor Ravinder Dahiya, head of the Bendable Electronics and Sensing Technologies (BEST) group based at the University of Glasgow's James Watt School of Engineering (University of Glasgow, 2020).

Tactile VR

Researchers from Northwestern University have developed a prototype device which aims to put touch within VR's reach, using a flexible material fitted with tiny vibrating components that can be attached to skin.

The system, known as epidermal VR, could be useful in other cases as well, from a child touching a display relaying the gesture to a family member located elsewhere, to helping people with amputations renew their sense of touch.

In gaming, it could alert players when a strike occurs on the corresponding body part of the game character.

The team's design features thirty-two vibrating actuators on a thin fifteen centimeter by fifteen centimeter silicone polymer which sticks on to the skin without tape or straps and is free of large batteries and wires.

It uses near-field communication (NFC) technology—which is used in many smartphones for mobile payment today—to transfer the data.

Scientists hope that the technology could eventually find its way into clothing, allowing people with prosthetics to wear VR shirts that communicate touch through their fingertips.

Putting Out Fire with Sound

Forest fires could one day be dealt with by drones that would direct loud noises at the trees below. Since sound is made up of pressure waves, it can be used to disrupt the air surrounding a fire, essentially cutting off the supply of oxygen to the fuel. At the right frequency, the fire simply dies out, as researchers at George Mason University in Virginia recently demonstrated with their sonic extinguisher. Apparently, bass frequencies work best.

Artificial Neurons on Silicon Chips

Scientists have found a way to attach artificial neurons onto silicon chips, mimicking the neurons in our nervous system and copying their electrical properties. "Until now neurons have been like black boxes, but we have managed to open the black box and peer inside," said Professor Alain Nogaret, from the University of Bath, who led the project. "Our work is paradigm-changing because it provides a robust method to reproduce the electrical properties of real neurons in minute detail. But it's wider than that, because our neurons only need 140 nanowatts of power. That's a billionth the power requirement of a microprocessor, which other attempts to make synthetic neurons have used." The researchers hope the technology could be used in medical implants to treat conditions such as heart failure and Alzheimer's as it requires so little power (PA News Agency, 2019).

Before we go to our last chapter, scan the QR code and check out 100 cool tech gadgets that, if nothing else, should inspire you on your journey to invent the next piece of technology that helps people enjoy life and complete jobs more easily.

10

Get a Job!

We've come to the end of our journey and the beginning of yours. Depending on what grade you're in, high school might be a few years away or just around the corner. Whatever the case, remember that you're never too young to come up with the next best invention that will turn the world upside down. In the meantime, the information in this chapter will give you a "heads-up" for what's down the road.

HIGH SCHOOL

When you get to high school you will start having the opportunity to take classes that help build a good knowledge base for your career in technology. High school students interested in a career in technology should take courses in programming and computer science. Other classes that will give you a solid foundation include algebra, trigonometry, geometry, chemistry and physics.

Another tip is to try and take Advanced Placement versions of these classes because a lot of high schools will give you college credit when you pass them!

Another bit of advice is to get involved. Whether it's a sport or band or clubs, the more you join in with these activities, the more practice you get of team building. When you are ready to go to college, you will be able to up the chances for scholarship money if you are able to say that you were involved.

DOI: 10.4324/9781003263142-10

COLLEGE

Next comes college. In this section we will explore a list of colleges that offer degrees that will open doors for your technology career as well as what colleges have related tech programs based on specific interests (US News Editors, 2022).

The colleges that have the top ranked programs for **technology** include:

1. Massachusetts Institute of Technology–Cambridge
2. California Institute of Technology–Pasadena
3. Georgia Technology Institute–Atlanta
4. Rensselaer Polytechnic Institute–Troy
5. Worcester Polytechnic Institute–Worcester
6. Virginia Tech–Blacksburg
7. Stevens Institute of Technology–Hoboken
8. Rochester Institute of Technology–Rochester
9. New Jersey Institute of Technology–Newark
10. Illinois Institute of Technology–Chicago

The colleges with the best programs for **application development** include (in order of rank) (US News Editors, 2022):

1. Massachusetts Institute of Technology–Cambridge
2. Stanford University–Stanford
3. Carnegie Mellon University–Pittsburgh
4. University of California–Berkeley
5. Harvard University–Cambridge
6. Princeton University–Princeton

The best colleges that will prepare you for a degree in **data science** include (US News Editors, 2022):

1. University of California–Berkeley
2. Carnegie Mellon University–Pittsburgh
3. Massachusetts Institute of Technology–Cambridge
4. Stanford University–Stanford
5. University of Washington–Seattle
6. Cornell University–Ithaca
7. Georgia Institute of Technology–Atlanta
8. Columbia University–New York
9. University of Illinois–Urbana-Champaign
10. University of Michigan–Ann Arbor

It's cool to see that a lot of the same colleges are on more than one of the lists! Sometimes people like to go to college close to home, while others don't mind going to a college far away in order to get the right education that matches their interests.

It would be fun if you printed out a map of the United States and find where you live and then use three different colors to mark the "technology" colleges, the "application development" colleges and the "data science" colleges. That will give you a great visual and a way to figure out how far away the colleges are from where you currently live!

...AND BEYOND

Finally, we've come to the end of our investigation of the electric world of technology. Be encouraged to revisit your notebook and add to your drawings and take more notes as you continue on your way through school. As you grow in knowledge, always be thinking ahead for solutions to problems. How can you use your talents to help people connect through the power of technology?

For fun, look at the world around you to see if something in nature can inspire your next idea. For example, the bullet train in Japan was modeled after the kingfisher bird to maximize its aerodynamic capabilities. The feet of geckos have inspired many technologies by the way they grab on to things, from space grippers that allow astronauts to make repairs in orbit to devices that let people climb glass walls.

Also consider how the animals around you helped people create new inventions. Velcro was invented when the creator saw his dog covered in sticker burrs and studied how the hooks on the burrs attached to the dog's fur. Shark skin is made to help the creature move through the water more quickly. Scientists at NASA were able to duplicate the skin pattern and create a special coating that was applied to boats to make them sail faster.

Don't forget about the plants all around you! Scientists are figuring out ways to use these to create new technologies to make life easier. Algae is being converted into fuel. There's a desert plant called guayule that people are using to make an alternative to latex—it's allergy free and a lot stretchier than traditional rubber. Corn is being used to make biodegradable plastics, while the lotus plant is being used to create water-repellant fabrics.

Wherever you turn for inspiration, don't forget that you can do great things. Use this book as a resource to revisit and keep learning about technology. Keep drawing and writing about your ideas in your notebook. You never know when they'll come in handy. Keep reading and researching. You are special and unique. You see things in ways that no one else does.

Before we finish, there's a crazy popular YouTuber named Lewis Hilsenteger. His channel is called Unbox Therapy and has over eighteen million subscribers and four billion views! Check it out by scanning the QR code and stay on top of the most current tech gadgets and trends around!

Take this guide to technology and dream about all the ways you can help others connect with the cool things that make the world turn. You're going to be amazed at what you can accomplish. Don't let anyone tell you you're not old enough or smart enough. Work hard in school and along the way look for connections between what you're learning and what you know about technology.

Microsoft founder Bill Gates said, "I spend a lot of time reading." Simple enough. Take his advice and use your time in school learning your subjects the best you can. Those are the small steps on your big path to an epic career in technology. Your future creations and inventions will be the giant leap that will take people everywhere to unknown places beyond the current advances in technology. It's exciting, isn't it? You've got this.

Good luck!

Works Cited

Apple Insider Staff. *Apple Park*. Appleinsider.com, January 28, 2022. Web.

Apple.com Editors. *Apple Watch Series 7*. Apple.com, October 4, 2021. Web.

Argonne National Laboratory. *How Your Smartphone Got Smart*. Anl.gov, September 13, 2013. Web.

Bellis, Mary. *History of the Computer*. ThoughtCo.com, July 3, 2019. Web.

Biography.com Editors. *Bill Gates*. Biography.com, April 2, 2022. Web.

Biography.com Editors. *Ginni Rometty*. Biography.com, April 2, 2022. Web.

Biography.com Editors. *Jeff Bezos*. Biography.com, April 2, 2022. Web.

Biography.com Editors. *Larry Page*. Biography.com, April 2, 2022. Web.

Biography.com Editors. *Mark Zuckerberg*. Biography.com, April 2, 2022. Web.

Biography.com Editors. *Sergey Brin*. Biography.com, April 2, 2022. Web.

Biography.com Editors. *Sheryl Sandberg*. Biography.com, April 2, 2022. Web.

Biography.com Editors. *Steve Jobs*. Biography.com, April 2, 2022. Web.

Biography.com Editors. *Susan Wojcicki*. Biography.com, April 2, 2022. Web.

Gianfagna, Mike. *What is Moore's Law?* Synopsys.com, June 30, 2021. Web.

Hanson, Heather. *The Evolution of Smartphones*. Blog.verb.tech, November 2, 2021. Web.

History Computer Staff. *Apple II Explained*. History-Computer.com, January 4, 2021. Web.

History.com Editors. *Invention of the PC.* History.com, May 11, 2011. Web.

Kukich, Diane S., McCullough, R.L., Girifalco, Louis A., Venables, John D., Patel, C., Kumar N. and Marchant, Roger Eric. "Materials Science." *Encyclopedia Britannica*, 22 March 2018. Web.

Mazer, Jeffrey. *Understanding the Cryptocurrency Market.* Toptal. com, 2022. Web.

Microsoft. *Amy Hood.* Microsoft.com, 2022. Web.

PA News Agency. *Hope for Cure of Chronic Diseases.* Centralfifetimes.com. December 3, 2019. Web.

Patel, Prachi. *Yarn-Like Rechargeable Zinc Could Power Smart Clothes.* Spectrum.leee.org, April 10, 2018. Web.

Perry, Caroline. "Radhika Nagpal, expert on swarm robotics, celebrated among 'Nature's 10.'" December 22, 2014. https://news.harvard.edu/gazette/story/newsplus/ radhika-nagpal-expert-on-swarm-robotics-celebrated-among-natures-10/Poly. *What Does Innovation Sound Like?* Blogs.poly.com, September 2, 2016. Web.

Riordan, Michael. "Transistor." *Encyclopedia Britannica*, March 26, 2020. Web.

ScienceFocus.com Editors. *Future Technology.* Sciencefocus.com, February 1, 2022. Web.

Swaine, Michael R. and Freiberger, Paul A. "ENIAC." *Encyclopedia Britannica*, January 31, 2022. Web.

University of Glasgow. *Working Up a Sweat Could Power Future Wearable Devices.* Gla.ac.uk. May 2020. Web.

US News Editors. *Best National University Rankings.* 2022. www. usnews.com/best-colleges/rankings/national-universities

Uswitch. *History of the Mobile Phone.* Uswitch.com, May 19, 2021. Web.

Valentine, Nick. *The History of the Calculator.* Thecalculatorsite. com, March 11, 2019. Web.

Williams, Geoff. *11 Best Technology Jobs in the US.* USNews.com, May 3, 2021. Web.

Zenco. *15 Engineers Building the Tech of the Future.* Zenco Technical, August 15, 2018. Web.

Printed in the United States
by Baker & Taylor Publisher Services